HORSE COLORING BOOK

ILLUSTRATIONS BY:
ANDREA MENDEZ

DREAM. INSPIRE. CREATE.

VISIT US ONLINE:
www.youngdreamerspress.com

TAG US IN YOUR PHOTOS & VIDEOS:
www.instagram.com/youngdreamerspress
www.tiktok.com/@youngdreamerspress

WE'RE ALSO ON FACEBOOK:
www.facebook.com/youngdreamerspress

ISBN-13: 978-1-990136-17-7

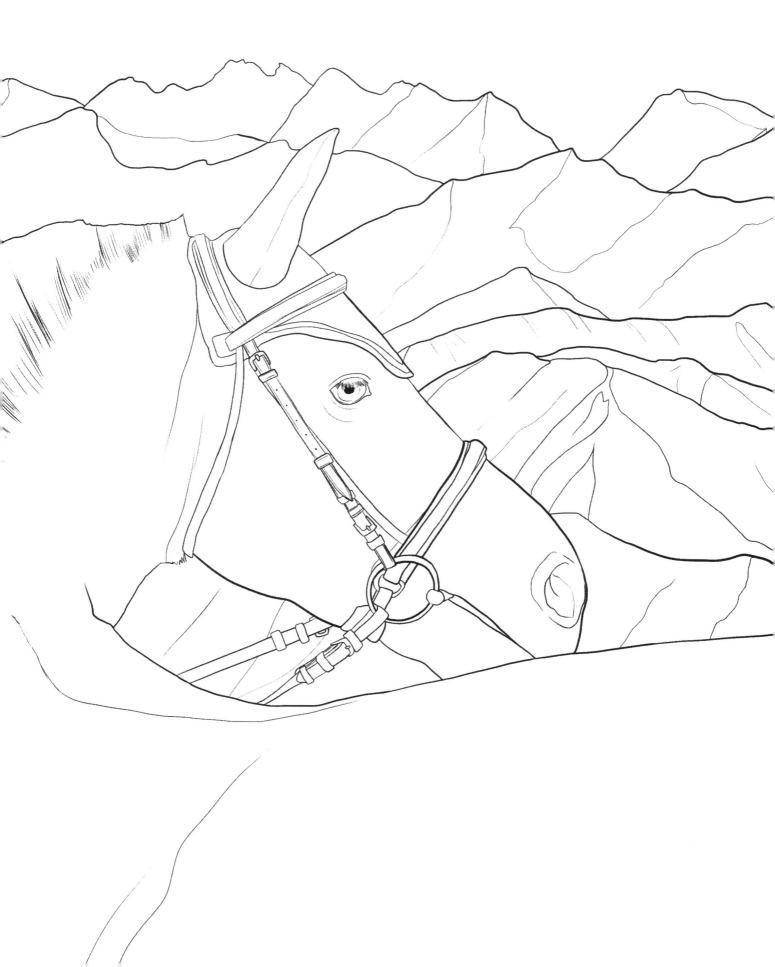

BUT WAIT, THERE'S MORE!

VISIT GO.YOUNGDREAMERSPRESS.COM/HORSES

To join our newsletter and
make their world more colorful with
free printable coloring pages!

All pages sized for 8.5 x 11 paper and include a wide
range of subjects including: animals, kittens,
mermaids, unicorns, mandalas, an astronaut, planets,
a firetruck, a construction vehicle, cupcakes, and more!

978-1-989387-13-9

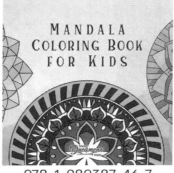

978-1-989387-46-7

978-1-989387-96-2

978-1-990136-07-8

978-1-990136-04-7

978-1-990136-05-4

978-1-989790-36-6

978-1-989790-96-0

Suitable for Ages 4-8 & 9-12

978-1-990136-06-1

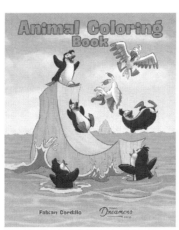

978-1-990136-09-2

978-1-990136-16-0

978-1-990136-13-4

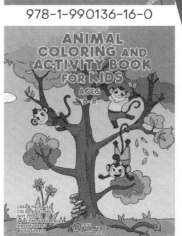

978-1-990136-02-3

978-1-989790-94-6

978-1-989790-69-4

978-1-990136-01-6

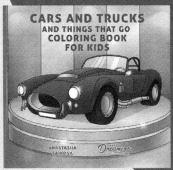

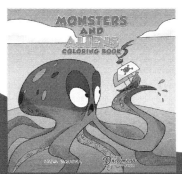

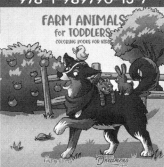

Manufactured by Amazon.ca
Bolton, ON